John Reeves

Addressed to the Quiet Good Sense of the People of England in a Series of Letters

Letter the First

John Reeves

Addressed to the Quiet Good Sense of the People of England in a Series of Letters
Letter the First

ISBN/EAN: 9783744716147

Printed in Europe, USA, Canada, Australia, Japan

Cover: Foto ©Suzi / pixelio.de

More available books at **www.hansebooks.com**

Thoughts on the English Government.

ADDRESSED TO THE

QUIET GOOD SENSE

OF THE

PEOPLE OF ENGLAND.

IN A SERIES OF LETTERS.

LETTER THE FIRST.

ON THE

National Character of Englishmen—The Nature of the English Government—The Corruptions caused in both by the Introduction of French Principles— The Effects produced by the Reformation and the Revolution upon Political Principles—The Conduct of the Whig Party—The Character of the modern Democrats.

LONDON:

PRINTED FOR J. OWEN, NO. 168, PICCADILLY.

1795.

[Price Two Shillings.]

TO THE READER.

THE following pages make part of what was intended as a Preface to a Work now in hand : But the Author having been gradually led into many reflections which are of a temporary nature, and fome of them fuch as may be thought not quite fuited to the temper and gravity of the Work to which they were to be prefixed, he gives them to the Public as a Pamphlet ; and if his manner of treating the fubject of our Government and Laws fhould be approved, the prefent fheets may be followed by more.

TO THE

QUIET GOOD SENSE

OF THE

PEOPLE OF ENGLAND.

I ADDRESS myfelf to you in that temper of
mind, which is produced when we contemplate
what may be confidered as the caufe of all the
happinefs we enjoy in this country.

GOOD SENSE is faid to be worth all learning and
all fcience ; and it is believed that, among other
diftinctions which we poffefs, in this Ifland, above
the Nations around us, we poffefs a great por-
tion of this excellent quality, through all ranks of
fociety, from the higheft to the loweft. I declare
myfelf one, who affents to this belief. Should any
of the modern philofophers, or politicians, think
this declaration too affuming and illiberal, and that

B   too

too little is allowed for the endowments and quali-
fications of the reft of mankind, my anfwer is this;
That I have not yet feen equal marks of Good Senfe
in thofe matters where of all others they fhould be
manifefted, I mean in their Laws and Government.
In the next place, I am not a *Citizen of the World*,
fo as to divide my affection with ftrangers—I am
an Englifhman—and I thank God for having
placed me among a People who, I think, poffefs
more goodnefs of heart and more GOOD SENSE than
any other in the world, and who are the happieft,
becaufe they make the beft ufe of both.

WHEN our happinefs fo much depends upon the
exercife of GOOD SENSE, how kind has Providence
been in beftowing this valuable quality fo generally through all ranks of People! It is to be found
among the middling and ordinary claffes as much
as among the higher; depending lefs upon the
helps of education than the original frame and
temperature of the mind. It is ufually diftinct
from the faculties that make moft fhow and attract
notice; it manifefts itfelf in conduct rather than
difcourfe; it is not what a man fays, fo much as
what he does. In fuch a fphere as this, how many
can act without feeming to be employed; and what
effects may be produced without any one appear-
ing to be in motion!

IT

It is in such quiet unperceived movements that the GOOD SENSE of the Country performs moſt of its operations, and exerciſes its influence on the conduct of public men and the national affairs. How often have we ſeen deſigns opened with high expectation, ſet off with great appearance of argument and much ornament of ſpeech! How have we ſeen parties combine; all their power of numbers, and all their arts of confederation brought into action! meeting after meeting! all the ſtirrers and all the talkers at work! no doubt of accomplifhing their object! no fuſpicion that anything could oppoſe them! and how have all theſe mighty doings been baffled, and ſcattered into air, without our ſeeing the hand that has deſtroyed them.

It is the GOOD SENSE of the Country that has done this; it is YOU who have confounded the builders in their mad work, and have difperfed them; one of them you have admoniſhed, another you have reprehended, another you have frowned down; all of them you have difcountenanced and difcredited; and behold! the leader and the led find no longer ſtrength in their numbers; their arguments appear to have no reafon, and their oratory no charms to miſlead.

Thus

THUS we generally find, that whatever actors may be on the stage, and whatever piece may be propofed, nothing can be brought to a fuccefsful conclufion unlefs it is approved by the GOOD SENSE of the Country; which, though it difcovers itfelf in a QUIET way, is very rarely without effect.

BEING fenfible of the final decifion YOU, fortunately for us, poffefs in all public matters, and wifhing publickly to own and fhew my reverence for the gentle and ufeful fway which you enjoy, and I hope will always maintain in this nation, I have addreffed to you thefe Thoughts upon the nature of our *Government*, which is now fafhionably called, *The Conftitution*. If my thoughts fhould be agreeable to YOUR GOOD SENSE, I fhall not doubt of their being founded on principles that are found, and truly Englifh.

THE peculiarities of the Englifh character are difcernible in nothing more than in the Laws and Government which they have gradually formed to themfelves. Thefe in their frame and quality, are entirely our own; and it is for want of our habit of thinking, that foreigners, who have ftudied them and are difpofed enough to admire them, do not yet comprehend their true value. We admire the fame things, but not in the fame manner, nor upon the fame motive, nor with the fame view.

Thus,

Thus, an Englishman loves *liberty*, but he loves
it not for the fake of the mere name; he muſt
have ſomething ſubſtantial that reſults from it;
ſomething that he can ſee and feel: this he has in
the freedom of his perſon, and the ſecurity of his
property. An Engliſhman, therefore, thinks
more of his *civil* than his *political* Liberty; more
of the end than the means: the conſequences of
the former are always before him, and he feels it
to be truly the Liberty he needs; the other is
only an occaſional reſource, a neceſſary evil, and
he ſees that the exerciſe of it too frequently tends
to private licentiouſneſs and public diſorder. ·

An Engliſhman is more *jealous* of Power, than
ambitious to partake of it. Thus he ſeeks not
to domineer over his neighbours, but he will take
good care, that they ſhall not domineer over him.
This jealouſy diſpoſes him more towards a *Mo-
narchical* than a *Republican* Government; for he
will bear with the ſuperiority of thoſe who are
his ſuperiors, but he will not brook, that his
equals ſhould be placed over him; and he feels
that the protection which his *civil* Liberty has
under the one ſort of Government, is a greater
bleſſing than all the ſway and honours that he
may chance to attain from the full exerciſe of
political Liberty in the other.

THESE

These qualities of the mind are joined with another, which has been noticed, and has fometimes raifed a fneer among foreigners. An Englifhman has a natural *modefty*, which is not unmixed with a quiet, referved, unaffuming *pride*. Thefe difpofe him to conform to fubordination, and to refpect rank and ftation : his modefty inclines him to yield that, which eftablifhed cuftom demands, and his pride will not allow him to affume what belongs to another. The native difpofition of Englifhmen, therefore, brings about imperceptibly that, which in other countries is prefcribed by pofitive inftitutions; I mean the diftinction of Ranks. But we poffefs this convenient modification of Society in a manner that is feen in no other country; for the diftinction of ranks with us makes no difference of perfons; we have no *privileged* Orders; and yet there are none of us who do not yield proper deference to diftinguifhed rank.——In no country, perhaps, is Nobility more efteemed and honoured; and yet certainly, when we confider what Nobility beftows on its poffeffors, in no country can it ftrike lefs awe, or need be lefs feared. We concede readily to them that refpect which we have the power to withhold; we unite in upholding the honour and influence of the higher ranks out of courtefy, and from a love of decorum;

rum; perhaps alfo from a confcioufnefs that many of us afpire, and a knowledge that all of us may by poffibility attain, to a participation of it, from fteady exertions and virtuous conduct.

This generofity in the middle and lower orders of life is not received by the Great without acknowledgment and return. To fay nothing of the relative fituation of the Nobleman and the Gentleman (where the famenefs of education and habits of life will not fuffer any effential diftinction of manners and fentiment), we feem, from the very higheft to the very loweft in the nation, to confefs that there is a native unalterable temper and conftitution of mind which belongs to us all in common; we exprefs it by two fhort words * that are at length become endeared to us; expreffing, as we all think, that original indelible character of an Englifhman; which the firft Nobleman is proud to profefs he enjoys, but enjoys only in common with the meaneft of his tradefmen, his tenants, or his fervants. This is a fentiment that makes us love and refpect one another. The want of this in France, where the Nobility and Gentry hated or defpifed thofe beneath them, as a diftinct race of men, was the

* John Bull

caufe

cause that they firſt placed barriers of ſeparation, which made an inequality that was invi-
dious ; and afterwards, in their rage to cure the
miſchief of ſuch a ſeparation, levelled all to an
equality that is more deteſtable than their former
diſtinctions. This feeling of a congenial equality
among us, is a philoſophy that is the growth of
this Iſland. Its riſe is natural, not forced ; it is
a philoſophy that comes from the heart, and not
from the head. It has been generated by a common conſent, not impoſed by hot-headed ſpecu-
lators ; and I truſt it will have the power to pre-
ſerve us by indiſſoluble bands of union, when the
artificial ſchemes of philoſophizing Politicians
are buried in oblivion.

But, above all things, an Engliſhman loves
Quiet.—*Gives us peace in our time*—is the language
of his prayers, and the ſilent wiſh of his heart.
How many virtues does this ſingle diſpoſition
oblige him to practiſe ! It is from hence that he
is patient and forbearing towards his Governors ;
not captious and wilful, but ſeeking the faireſt
conſtruction of what they do ; aſcribing to them
the ſame honeſty of intention which he feels in
his own mind. And, ſhould his jealouſy once be
excited, he will bear and forbear for a time, ſtill
hoping that things may mend. He knows the
value

value of what he poffeffes better, than lightly or haftily to wifh for a change, and he dreads every change may be for the worfe. What ftorms and convulfions have been efcaped by the prevalence of this love for *Peace* and *Quiet !* But the more immediate confequence of it is this, that its kindred quality GOOD SENSE has thus an interval left, to interpofe its protecting influence, and confider of fuch remedies as may feem fuited to the nature of the exifting evil.

THE Englifh Government is an organ of public union and activity, which is adapted to the humour and mode of thinking of thofe who were witneffes to the formation of it, and who live under it. It appears to me, we may difcern in the whole difpofition of it, the refult of that conftitution of mind which I have juft afcribed to our countrymen. Unambitious, and preferring the quiet and peace, which enables them to purfue their own affairs, to the power and fplendor of managing thofe of the public, the Englifh yield a willing obedience to a Government not of their own chufing: it is an Hereditary King, who bears all the burthen of Government, who is endued with all the power neceffary to carry it on, and who enjoys all the honour and pre-eminence neceffary to give fplendor to fo high a ftation. It is the *King's Peace,* under

C   which

which we enjoy the freedom of our perfons and the fecurity of our property : he *makes*, and he *executes* the Laws, which contain the rules by which that peace is kept ; and for this purpofe, all officers, civil and military, derive their authority from him. Still further to ftrengthen this all-powerful fway, two qualities are added that feem to bring this Royal Sovereignty, as far as mortal inftitutions can be, ftill nearer to the Government of Heaven. Firft, This Power is to have perpetual continuance—*the King never dies.*— Secondly, Such unbounded power fhall be prefumed to be exercifed with as eminent goodnefs ; and it is accordingly held that—*the King can do no wrong* ;—meaning, that his perfon is fo facred that wrong fhall never be imputed to him.

THESE are the original and main principles upon which the plain Englifhman, full of honefty and confidence, thinks he may reft for the protection of his perfon and property. But human inftitutions will fwerve from their original defign, and Englifhmen will not always confide ; jealoufies and fears arife, and thofe muft be appeafed. The reafonable jealoufy of an Englifhman feems to be fully fatisfied, when a qualification is annexed to the power in the King, firft, of *making*, and fecondly, of *executing* the Laws ; by which his

fubjects

fubjects are admitted to participate in a fhare of thofe high trufts.

ACCORDINGLY, the King can *enact* no Laws without *the advice and confent*, not only of *the Lords Spiritual and Temporal*, who are in fome fort counfellors of his own chufing, but alfo of *the Commons in Parliament affembled*. And the jealoufy with regard to property has been fuch, that in devifing this meafure the fubject has fuffered a guard to be put upon himfelf; for the *Commons*, who are to advife and confent, are not the people at large, nor are they chofen by the people at large, but they are the *Knights*, *Citizens*, and *Burgeffes*, who are refpectively chofen in *Counties*, *Cities*, and *Boroughs*, by perfons of fubftance and fufficiency, who may fafely be trufted with the exercife of a charge where property is in queftion.

IN this manner is the power of the King qualified in the *making* of Laws. His power in *executing* the Laws is qualified by joining Grand and Petty Juries, in the adminiftration of Juftice, with his Judges. To thefe two controuls on the power of the King, muft be added a principle, which gives the Nation another fecurity for the due exercife of the Kingly Power; for though the King can do no wrong, yet if wrong is done by the application of the King's

Power,

Power, as he never acts without advice, the per-
son who advises such application is responsible to
the Law.

With the exception, therefore, of the advice
and consent of the Two Houses of Parliament, and the interposition of Juries; the Government, and the administration of it in all its
parts, may be said to rest wholly and solely on
the King, and those appointed by him. Those
two adjuncts of *Parliament* and *Juries* are sub-
sidiary and occasional; but the King's Power is
a substantive one, always visible and active.
By his Officers, and in his name, every thing is
transacted that relates to the peace of the Realm
and the protection of the Subject. The Subject
feels this, and acknowledges with thankfulness
a superintending sovereignty, which alone is congenial with the sentiments and temper of Englishmen. In fine, the Government of England is *a
Monarchy*; the Monarch is the antient stock from
which have sprung those goodly branches of the
Legislature, the Lords and Commons, that at the
same time give ornament to the Tree, and afford
shelter to those who seek protection under it.
But these are still only branches, and derive their
origin and their nutriment from their common
parent; they may be lopped off, and the Tree

is a Tree ſtill; ſhorn indeed of its honours, but not, like them, caſt into the fire. The Kingly Government may go on, in all its funƈtions, without Lords and Commons : it has heretofore done ſo for years together, and in our times it does ſo during every receſs of Parliament ; but without the King *his* Parliament is no more. The King, therefore, alone it is who neceſſarily ſubſiſts, without change or diminution : and from *him* alone we unceaſingly derive the protec-tion of Law and Government.

Such are the Principles and Conſtitution of the Engliſh Government delivered down to us from our anceſtors ; ſuch they can be demonſtrated to be from the inconteſtible evidence of hiſtory and records ; and ſuch it is wiſhed they ſhould continue by nine tenths of the Nation.

But, notwithſtanding this great· majority. in favour of the Government, there have never been wanting perſons to find fault with it, decry its excellence, and do their endeavours to ſubvert it, and ſet up another in its place. Though ſuch perſons err againſt the plaineſt evidence, yet, all circumſtances conſidered, it is not to be wondered that differences of this ſort ſhould happen under a Government, whoſe beſt title is profeſſed to be,

4   its

its conformity to the principles of reafon; it is not to be wondered that this, among other fub-jects, fhould occafionally become matter of fpe-culation, and be brought to the teft which it fo readily challenged. And, where liberty of fpeech and of writing has been fo invariably al-lowed, this fpirit of difcuffion could not fail of fpreading. Thus, from the beft of motives, might the merits of our Laws and Government be brought in queftion. Little mifchief could be dreaded from honeft difputations like this, and ultimately fome benefit might be derived from the new lights, which frequent argumentation would be fure of producing. The opponents, in fuch controverfies, might be friendly to the Government equally with the defendants: differ-ing in the means, and not in the end; in circum-ftances, and not in the fubftance.

But the greater part of thofe who have raifed queftions upon the merits of our Government, are certainly determined enemies to its fundamental principles; and amongft thefe are fome, who have moft affumed the guife and affectation of great friends and favourers of *The Conftitution.* That there fhould be perfons of this defcription is not much more to be wondered than that there fhould be miftaken friends of the defcription before mentioned.

THE

THE truth is, that all Englifhmen are not of the ftamp I have above fuppofed to belong to our Countrymen. But thofe who bear a different mark feem to me to be influenced by a defect of mind, which I muft confider as an aberration from the national character and general difpofition of Englifhmen. In thefe men, it is fometimes the underftanding, and fometimes the will that has received a wrong bias; either their affections are hurried away by an impreffion from ftrong propenfities, that they think too well juftified to need examination; or their underftandings are fo fophifticated by preconceived opinions, that they are unable to make a clear judgment of any thing that is to affect thofe opinions: fo that by the ftrength of the will, or the weaknefs of the wit, they go on from error to error, and are almoft always in a heat from the purfuit, and from the difappointment attending it.

SUCH are thofe men, who contrary to the genius of Englifhmen, hate *peace* and *quiet*, and inftead of repofing themfelves confidently on the Government of the King, earneftly feek to have a fhare in it themfelves. Such men have ufually no calling of their own, or none that they attend, and they wifh to make one for themfelves in the affairs of the public. Such are thofe unbridled

fpirits

fpirits that hate all power but their own, and would cry down all rank and ftation that they may rife upon its downfall, leaving no inequality in the land but the wealth they appropriate from the fpoil of the good and great; who would rather take the chance to become one of five hundred Republicans that govern by their ordinances, that is, by their own will, than continue the fubjects of a King who governs by Law. It is not to be expected, that men blinded by paffion, and ftimulated to defigns fo contrary to the general bent of the Englifh character, fhould be influenced by any fuggeftions of that GOOD SENSE, which prevails fo much with the reft of their country-men. Delivered over to a ftate of reprobation, they act as totally bereaved of that fpecies of faving and preventive grace, which interpofes its admonitions fo feafonably, and fo often refcues us from the commiffion of fome folly or wickednefs.

WHEN we find, amongft a fober and difcreet people, a certain fet with crazed brains and per-verted underftandings oppofing their own conceits to the general inclination of the people, we are led to enquire what could have been the caufe of fuch a fchifm, whence the fpirit originated, and what motives or encouragement could have confpired to keep it up. And here I feel fome confolation

confolation to be able to fay, that although the
difpofition to cavil at our Laws and Government,
and to extol another fyftem, is a mifchief that
has been cherifhed and ftrengthened by the ma-
licious induftry of many amongft ourfelves; yet
it is a weed of foreign original, tranfplanted by
men who had fuffered their minds to be captivated
and corrupted by outlandifh fafhions; and only
adopted and cultivated here by perfons of a light
or fanatical humour, addi&ed to paradox, infa-
tuated with refinement, and fond of innovation.

It is from a nation whofe national chara&er is
the very oppofite to ours, that the feeds of this
evil were borrowed, and then fcattered in this
ifland; a nation, which has made itfelf odious to
Europe by its violence and fraud; always planning frefh hoftility againft its neighbours, either
by arms and open war, or by fomenting internal
commotions : and by fuch bafe means this
Nation has grown to a fize and importance that
the Great Difpenfer of all things has not feen fit in
his wifdom to allow to thofe, who confine themfelves within the facred bounds of juftice, and
propofe nothing but the fafety of themfelves and
the peace of mankind;—a Nation, which the fame
juft God has neverthelefs at length punifhed for
its iniquities, by delivering them over to their
own vain and wicked imaginations, fo that they

D   might

might revenge upon themſelves the injuries of Europe, more by a thouſand fold, than all Europe itſelf could have done; and that they might become a ſcorn and by-word for every thing hateful and abominable among men:—a Nation ſo unfit for the enjoyment of liberty, that while they were kept in ſubjection to their Kings they had Religion and Laws, manners and refinement, and were admired and imitated by their neighbours; but, ſince they have broken from that reſtraint, and have recovered what they call Liberty, they have pulled down and aboliſhed all thoſe valuable ſupports of life, even to the very wreck of civilization itſelf. In *their* place, their Rulers have erected one mockery of a Conſtitution after another; haranguing daily upon Liberty, but exerciſing the moſt unexampled Oppreſſion; for Oppreſſion is ſtill the lot of a Frenchman. In a Republic of three years ſtanding, the greateſt exploit they have to boaſt is the deſtroying of a tyranny that filled upfift een months of the time. And who was this tyrant? Not a man on an eſtabliſhed throne, ſurrounded with guards, and abetted by powerful alliances and numerous friends and dependants; it was one of themſelves, who ſhewed himſelf daily among them, of the ſame order, upon the ſame form.

WHAT

. WHAT a counterfeit of Liberty has been played off upon the poor people of that country! and what a degenerate down-trodden race muſt they be, who have not diſcovered the impoſition ; or, diſcovering it, have not reſiſted it, and done themſelves juſtice ! this could not be, if there was any honeſty, any fortitude, or any manly ſentiment in the country ; but theſe are not qualities to be found in France, and Liberty ſeems deſtined never to make her abode there. Men muſt be trained to Liberty; and a whole Nation cannot ſo eaſily practiſe it as a Committee of conceited Academicians can lay down definitions, and propound maxims for its eſtabliſhment. The mind and manners of a Frenchman need much purifying, before he can comprehend the Liberty he talks of with ſo much fluency and heat. Liberty is the reward of thoſe only who are juſt and good; and it is to be attained only by thoſe who have GOOD SENSE enough to underſtand it, and to uſe it with moderation.

BUT, although the French nation have miſ-carried in the only attempt they ever made to eſtabliſh Liberty in their own country, they have, neverthelefs, produced men, who in their writings have endeavoured to advance a *cauſe* which bore the appearance of it ; and ſome, who have been

able

able actually to carry it into practice in other countries. In former times, thofe who fled from flavery at home became Apoftles of Liberty abroad; and fince the Nation has perfuaded itfelf that the land is full of Liberty, the eftab-lifhing a college for *propagating* their bleffed doctrines in foreign countries, is nothing more than might be expected from the vainglory of a Frenchman. Be the times what they may, the Governments of Europe are ftill to be difturbed with the conceits of Frenchmen! Whether it is for Religious or Civil Liberty, they will never keep their inventions to themfelves; they are determined, by preaching and profelyting, to bring all the world to conform to the new lights which they alone have difcovered ; and to infult the blindnefs and folly of thofe who refift their fraternization! From *Calvin* down to *Condorcet*, from *Beza* to *Briffot* (innovators in different mat-ters, but alike in the felf-fufficiency, heat, and imperioufnefs belonging to all Frenchmen), no true Gofpel but theirs ; no *Rights of Man* but theirs ; no Government in *Church* or *State* but according to their *platform* and their principles.

We all know the deftructive doctrines upon which the French Liberty of the prefent day is founded; and we fee, with uneafinefs, the pains

and

and the fuccefs in propagating them in this Country. The infection has fpread already too far; and, fuch is the fatal feduction of thofe principles, that they are too likely to work their way much further: their loofenefs is likely to win to their fide the diffolute and immoral; their fpecioufnefs to enfnare the unwary and unprepared; men of bad principles find a comfort and fupport in them; men of no principles know not how to combat them. Thus it has happened, that many of our countrymen, who had not ftrongly impreffed on their minds the National Character before defcribed, have given themfelves up to thefe foreign delufions, and have begun to apply them to the reforming and newmodelling of the antient Government eftablifhed in this Land by the wifdom and experience of our forefathers.

SUCH is the *prefent* novelty from France! We may learn from Hiftory what was the nature of the principles which *Calvin* and *Beza*, and their followers at Geneva, inftilled into the *Puritans*, who infefted our Government in the reign of Queen Elizabeth; and who, under the name of *Prefbyterians, Commonwealth's-men, Independents,* and other factions and fects without number, at length overturned firft the Government of Scotland, and afterwards the Government of England.

4 Upon

Upon examination we shall find a similar spirit prevailing in the French principles of those days, and of the present times.

It would be curious to pursue the comparison that sometimes makes a contrast, and sometimes a parallel, between the character and designs of the French Reformers of old time in the Church, and those of the present day in the State; the Religious and the Civil *Jacobins*; the *Puritans*, and the *Democrats*. It is wonderful how similar they all are in their doctrines, and how they agree in the system and the instruments they use for disseminating their principles, for gaining proselytes, and for *carrying on* the unhallowed *work* of setting the populace against the established Government. How analogous was the machinery of their party; the cant and imposture of their pretences!—— The unalienable rights of the People to form the Government of the Church, taught by *Calvin* and the *Puritans*; and the unalienable right of the People to form the Government of the State, taught by the *French Democrats* :——The pretended commands of God for the one; and that omnipotent power upon earth, the Sovereign Will of the People commanding the other.—— What is "The sword of the Lord and of Gideon" but the modern title to the holy right of infur-
rection?

rection ? View the Covenants and Engagements of the one, the Civic Oaths of the other ; both alike sworn, and broken and re-sworn ;—the hypocrisy of Solemn Fasts, and the mummery of Civic Feasts ;—the Classes and Conventicles of the one, and the Affiliated Clubs of the other ;—the Pulpit, and the Tribune——preaching down, or lecturing down the Government ;—affected appellations of Brethren and Citizens ;—and, lastly, the spring of action that is the cause of motion in the two, the Fanaticism of those who had too much sense of Religion, and the illumination and New Lights of the latter, who have no Religion at all.

In making this comparison, I have taken the liberty to mix together the character and proceedings of the French abroad, as well as of their disciples in this country ; it is all a part and result of the same system. The first French Reformers, and their followers in this Country, proclaimed a Church Government, which was the invention of *Calvin*'s brain, as commanded by God, and as imposing upon every one the obligation to overturn the established Church Government, and erect this in its place ; such was the impudence and profanation of the *Puritans.* The modern French Reformers declare all Government

ment to be ufurpation which is not formed by the
will of the People; and that the People have an
imprefcriptible right to fubvert fuch Government and make another according to their own
will and pleafure; fuch are the imperious pretenfions of the *Jacobins.* The principles of the
Puritans and the *Jacobins* equally tend to fedition
and rebellion, and equally ftrike us with terror:
the one refted its fupport on the greateft Power in
Heaven, and the other depends upon the greateft
Power on Earth: the witneffes vouched for thefe
high demands, feem to be equally fufpicious in
both; they are to be found nowhere but in the in-
fcrutable ways of their own minds; in their own
ftrong perfuafions, dazzled by vain imaginations,
and ftrengthened by the confirmation of . felf-
will.

In order to fee the manner in which French
principles have iufinuated themfelves into this
Ifland, and vitiated the plain honefty of the
Englifh charaéter, it will be neceffary to look
back to fome occurrences in our Hiftory. We
fhall then fee what pretences have been ufed,
from time to time, to bring our antient Laws and
Government into difcredit, and to corrupt their
genuine principles with notions introduced from
abroad, and no lefs foreign in their nature than
their original.

It feems to me, that moft of the errors and mifconceptions relative to the nature of our Government, have taken their rife from thofe two great events, *The Reformation*, and what is called *The Revolution*. There has either been fome diffatisfaction with the manner and extent of thofe two meafures, or fome mifapprehenfion of their defign, or a want of infight into the grounds and principles of the fubject matter, namely, the Government in Church and State.

Those memorable tranfactions were conducted in a way that was truly Englifh; the actors in them proceeded with their remedy as far as the difeafe reached, and no further; and they never fuffered themfelves to lofe fight of this main rule, that what they did was to preferve the antient Government, and not to deftroy or alter it.

By the Reformation, it was intended to remove thofe errors and fuperftitions that had gradually been introduced into the doctrines and ceremonies of the Church by the Popifh Clergy; fo that Chriftianity might be profeffed in that purity and fimplicity which prevailed in the primitive ages. At the fame time, occafion was taken to put an end to the long-contefted claim of the Pope to exercife ecclefiaftical dominion over the King's

E   fubjects

subjects in this kingdom. The whole of that usurped jurisdiction was expressly and completely taken away by Act of Parliament; and that jurisdiction, first under the name of *Headship*, and then of *Supremacy in all Ecclesiastical Matters*, was placed by the same authority in the King. The Church was thus fast bound to the Monarchy; and this union of all authority, ecclesiastical as well as civil, in the Crown, it was hoped, besides placing Religion out of danger, would make a common cause between Church and State, would produce mutual advantages to both, and give to the antient pillar of the Government, the Crown, new strength and splendor for the protection of the subject.

Thus much and no more seems to have been the sum of what was done and designed to be done by the Reformation. The first observation that is suggested by this event is, upon the wonderful moderation that seems to have prevailed through the whole. It is a master-piece of temper and good sense, and will ever remain an example, among several others, of the great wisdom shewn by our Churchmen, and the services they have done, at different times, towards preserving our antient Government.

THE

The conduct and fuccefs of our Reformation becomes more ftriking when we look abroad and take a view of the proceedings of our neighbours in the fame fort of work. A fpirit of diffatisfaction had fpread in France on the fubject of Popifh fuperftitions. According to the difpofition for caballing and profelyting fo remarkable in that people, opinions engendered in France were foon preached and propagated at Geneva, and through the Seventeen Provinces of the Netherlands; countries ftill deftined to be infefted either by. French arms, or by French principles, which generate internal diftractions that are worfe than war. In all thefe countries, except in France itfelf, the people took the affair of Reformation into their own hands, and, proceeding in the only way of reforming underftood by them, they began to pull down and overturn every thing that had been eftablifhed in the Church; believing that nothing could be primitive Chriftianity that was not wholly oppofite to the fyftem which they had been ufed to, and was now condemned. Thefe commotions were fuppreffed in fome of the Provinces; but in the others, and at Geneva, they became the actual ground-work of the Reformation that was afterwards fettled.

THE

THE Bishop and Clergy of Geneva, like many others of their order, had fled, to escape the fury of the populace. At this crisis, the French refugee *Calvin* happening to come to that town was chosen by the people to be their pastor. Having once got a footing, he succeeded, not without some vicissitudes, and through many a shift and artifice, to establish and maintain to his death over the people who raised him, an ascendancy which they neither liked nor dared to shake off. From this time, Geneva became the school for teaching the new opinions in doctrine and Church government; and during the unfortunate interval of persecution in the reign of Queen Mary, many of our exiled Reformers took up their residence in that place, and there imbibed those notions which afterwards wrought so much confusion and misery in this Island.

As *Calvin* came into power on no authority but that of the people, he could form his Church government upon no other than popular principles. He joined, therefore, two elders with the Minister, and gave to these parochial officers supreme authority in all Church matters, without appeal, except in special cases: and thus he subjected the whole community of a parish to the direction of three persons, two of them laymen of an ordinary

stamp,

ftamp, who were likely to fubmit their judgment in moſt things to the guidance of their ſpiritual aſſociate. This ſpecies of Government was pro-feſſed to be ſuch as God had commanded for the government of his Church, and ſuch as all were bound in conſcience to ſet up, againſt all op-poſition, whether from Magiſtrates, Biſhops, or Kings.

WHEN this popular baſis for Church government had once taken full poſſeſſion of the mind, it was not likely ſoon to ceaſe fermenting. The work of Reformation is very apt to overheat thoſe who are engaged in it; the bold ſpirit of ſuch *projectors* grows bolder as they go on; every ſucceſs gives new courage; and if they have the ſtrong hand of the people to ſecond them, what ſhould ſtop their ambitious deſigns. We accordingly find, that the *French* Reformers of the Church ſoon undertook to ſearch into the title of the Civil Magiſtrate, and examine by what authority and upon what truſt he exerciſed his power. They ſoon told him, that the origin of all power was from the People; and they began to threaten Sovereign Princes with the ſame tremendous ſtorm which had been blown up againſt the Biſhops. Indeed, they did not open this attack without well knowing what they had to depend upon. The populace (who upon ſuch oc-caſions are called the People) were a monſter which

theſe

thefe Minifters had in their own tuition and keeping; they knew they could work upon their fanatical fancies as ferved their purpofe; could heat
them and cool them, unbridle and bridle them,
as they pleafed. In this manner did a new fet of
opinions ftart up to fhake the peace of fociety;
and Civil Authority was once more expofed to be
undermined by the plots and confederations of
Churchmen, carrying on their work under the
pretence of religion.

THE Princes of Europe had weathered the ftorms
that ufed to be directed againft them from the
Papal Throne; and the thunder of excommunica-
tion or deprivation no longer daunted the Prince,
becaufe the People no longer thought it a pretence for rebellion: but the new opinions gave
more alarm than any danger that had been efcaped.
The People were now tempted to rebellion, not
becaufe their Prince was excommunicated, and the
Pope authorifed them fo to do, but becaufe they
believed themfelves the origin of all Civil Authority. So long as Man loves himfelf, and is fond
of his own will and imaginations, fo long will he
liften with gratification to fuch doctrines. Thefe
puritanical notions give a zeft to fedition and a
title to rebellion which could never be difcovered
in any Papal Bull; and accordingly, wherever
they

they were brought into action, they were accompanied with a rage and ferociousness that is peculiar to Fanaticism, whether in a *Puritan* or a *Jacobin*.

THESE notions upon Civil Government are to be found in the writings of *Calvin* and *Beza*, and in those of *Buchannan*, *John Knox*, *Cartwright*, and others of the Geneva Discipline, who chose to make this Island the Theatre for acting some of their Tragedies.

THE praise of moderation and wisdom before bestowed on the English Reformers I cannot help repeating here, when I turn my eyes to the sad confusion caused in the sister kingdom by a contrary conduct. Unhappily, the people there took into their own hands the affair of Reformation, and it was performed to a degree of subversion and anarchy, that could only be suggested by fanaticism, and executed by popular fury. More unhappily for that country, and ultimately for this, the seditious spirit then infused by *Puritanism* was not allayed for many years after; during which the *Presbyterians* in Scotland had an opportunity, by co-operating with their brethren in this kingdom, to become the principal cause of the rebellion in the time of Charles the First, which

led

led to abolifhing, firft the Church Ceremonies and Government by Bifhops (the immediate objeft of all their deteftation), and afterwards the Houfe of Lords and the King, who, I firmly believe, will in no times be able long to furvive the firft breach made in the fabric of Civil and Ecclefiafti- cal Government.

In the midft of the confufion and anarchy that reigned in the neighbouring countries where Reformation was going on, the Church of England had reafon to congratulate herfelf that this great work had been accomplifhed with all the forms of law in a parliamentary way, and that fhe was united with the interefts of the Crown in fuch manner as to claim the full fupport of the Civil Power, if affailed by enemies ; and further fhe might comfort herfelf, that her reforms were fo temperate, and fo compatible with all the effentials of the late ftate of the Church, that her enemies would be few, and thofe few would have little ftrength of reafon for maintaining their oppofition. For feveral years of the early part of Queen Eli- zabeth's reign the Church enjoyed peace, not- withftanding the Papift *was ftill in the land.*

But now was the time for a new adverfary to appear, more implacable and politic than even

the

the Papift, and one too fprung from the bofom of Reformation itfelf. Many of the Englifh who had fuffered their minds to be infected with Calviniftical opinions during their refidence in Geneva and in the Low Countries, began, about the year 1572, to complain of our Reformation as incomplete; and from that time men of this perfuafion never ceafed, by their writings and conduct, to manifeft-the moft violent diflike of· our Church, and to profefs openly their wifh and defign to overtuin it and fet up the difcipline of Geneva in its place. Doctrines like thefe were · very alarming, becaufe they were levelled not only againft the Bifhops, who were a confiderable part of the Legiflature, but againft the fupremacy fo lately united to the Crown. Such is the effect of all extremes, that the Calviniftical Church, no lefs than the Popifh, affumed to itfelf to be independent of the Civil Magiftrate, and thus threatened to revive all the inconvenience of a power in the Church diftinct from that of the State; an *imperium in imperio* fo ill brooked in the Pope'; and the fettling of which in the Crown was thought to be one of the happieft ftrokes in the Reformation. In this point of the Supremacy they were therefore joined by the Papifts, and both parties thought their objections particularly ftrengthened at that time, from the circumftance

F   of

of the Throne being filled by a Woman. But though the Crown was, in this particular, affailed by both parties, and although the *Puritans*, in other refpects, never ceafed heaping upon their brother Non-Conformifts, the Papifts, every odium that could be invented, and endeavoured, by keeping up this cry, to draw off the attention of the Government from their own defigns, they were, nevertheléfs, regarded all through the remainder of this reign, by thofe who, it appears fince, faw fartheft into human affairs, as the faction moft of all to be dreaded, on account of their principles, and the activity, perfeverance, and fyftem with which they promoted them.

THE high pretenfions of this *new difcipline* did not pafs without moft complete anfwers in point of argument. The writings of *Whitgift*, of *Bancroft*, and more particularly of *Hooker*, had fo fully examined and confuted every argument alledged for the propofed Reformation, and fo expofed the pernicious tendency of the new doctrines, and the dangerous defigns which the authors of them meditated, and which they had actually begun to put in practice, that they were completely filenced by the end of this reign; fo that at the commencement of the next reign, in the conference at Hampton Court, held in the

prefence

'prefence of King James, they „could make no
'fhow of defence whatfoever.

But though the *Puritans* were fo foiled in argument, they did not, on that account, relinquifh their
purpofe. The failure, indeed, in the conference,
feemed to have this effect, that they no longer pretended to force their difcipline into notice upon
any open and bold claim of merit in its favour,
but thenceforward rather confined themfelves
to raifing and keeping up a cry about the increafe
of Papifts and the danger of Popery. In the mean
while, they loft no time filently to improve every
opportunity for fpreading their opinions, and adding
to the number of their difciples and partizans.

During the reign of James and Charles the
Firft, other matter of public diffatisfaction arofe,
which the *Puritans* could manage with better face
than their own ecclefiaftical pretenfions; and if
they could work any political differences up to a
pitch of general difcontent, and fo to refiftance
againft the Government, their end would be
equally ferved, and their darling object might
ftand a chance of being attained without directly
contending for it. It is well known, that both in
Parliament and out of Parliament the moft forward to quarrel with the meafures of Government,

F 2   and

and to foment contention between the Crown and the People, were thofe infected with *Puritanical opinions.* This conteft went on from bad. to worfe, till the plot was thoroughly matured, and the whole broke out into full-blown rebellion in the year 1641. This was not brought to bear till the Scots army of *Prefbyterian Covenantors* was prevailed upon to invade the kingdom, and our Houfe of Commons recognized and received with open arms their *Puritanical Brethren;* then the *Covenant* was taken univerfally by the Parliament and all its adherents; the long-looked-for time was arrived, when *Calvin's* plan of Church government—*Prefbytery by Divine Right*—was to be erected on the ruins of Epifcopacy; and it was accordingl fo ordained by the Parliament.

We all know what followed; and the calamities endured by the unhappy people for near twenty years, till the Country, worn out with projects of one Government after another, in none of which was found fecurity of property, freedom of perfon, or the peace and quiet it fo much fighed after, at length recovering its good fenfe and former energy, returned to the place whence it had fo fatally departed, and caufed, without bloodfhed or a blow, the antient Government of Monarchy to be reftored in 1660.

Such

Such were the viciffitudes and cataftrophe attending the firft fet of *French opinions* introduced into this kingdom, for the purpofe of difparaging, undermining, and fubverting the Conftitution of our Government eftablifhed by law. They fet out with a frivolous exception to Caps and Surplices worn by Minifters in performance of Divine Service; they proceeded to cavil at the government of the Church by Bifhops, and at placing that Supremacy in the Crown, which ought, as they contended, to refide in the Parfon of the parifh and his two Lay elders. Not being able to advance this by argument, or win the people to a liking of the defign, they referved themfelves to take advantage of every occafion to public difcontent, and became the moft forward Patriots of the time; till they were enabled, under pretence of the general good, for preferving the People's rights and maintaining the good old laws of the country, as they faid, to deftroy all ranks and ftations in Church and State; to levy war againft the King, for the protection, as they pretended, of the King's perfon; and, finally, to deftroy him: all which they tranfacted under various denominations of *Prefbyterians, Independents, Commonwealth's men, Fifth Monarchy Men, Anabaptifts, Quakers,* and other fects and divifions too irkfome to be named; all of them, more or lefs, difciples of the fame school;

school; where the Sovereignty of the people and the Killing of Kings was firft brought into fyftem, and fanctioned by the dictates of the Gofpel.

THE abdication of King James the Second, and the tranfactions that enfued upon the vacancy thereby made in the Throne, compofe a very important and curious paffage in the Hiftory of our Government and Laws. It has been vulgarly called, *The Revolution;* upon what authority I know not; it was not fo named by Parliament, nor is it a term known to our Laws. This term had certainly no better origin than the converfa-tion and pamphlets of the time, where words are ufed, in a popular and hiftorical fenfe, without any regard or thought of technical propriety. But, unfortunately, this invention, or mifapplica-tion of words, leads to a confufion of ideas; knowledge is thereby put into a retrograde courfe; inftead of going from things to words, we are obliged to pafs from words to things: let the term *Revolution* be once confecrated as the true denomination of that event, and the mind afcribes to that tranfaction every thing which it can conceive to belong to the term. Too many among us ufe the word in fome fuch indeterminate general fenfe, and fuch perfons are accordingly mif-led by notions that have no fort of connexion with the

3.

the thing of which they are fpeaking : and yet it is
remarkable, that thofe who embrace this phantom
do it with a zeal and prepoffeffion which we do not
fee in thofe who regard the fubftance and reality.
Thefe men think they can never fhew fufficient
warmth and emotion when they name *The Revolution ;* they form Clubs to fwear by, and wor-
fhip it ; they make great feafts to celebrate it ;
they have no love for *The Conftitution* but for that
which was *formed at the Revolution ;* and they are
good fubjects and loyal, only upon *Revolution
principles.*

WHAT can be the caufe of this mighty zeal ?
Whence does it originate, and to what does it
tend ?—This beloved Revolution happened more
than a century ago ; fo that all the heat which
naturally attends fuch a crifis, and which may be
kept up while it was recent, muft have long fince
cooled and died away. No one can fay, that any
of the caufes which produced that event, have re-
curred in our time, fo as to remind us of the
remedies our anceftors applied on that occafion,
All this earneft demonftration of affection and
devotion, without any apparent caufe or occafion.
is either ridiculous affectation, or fignifies fomething that is not obvious to perfons of common
underftandings. For we may afk them, Who has
cenfured

cenfured or cavilled at thofe proceedings, that fhould move thefe perfons fo violently to defend or extol them? And we may further afk, Who befides themfelves fay or think any thing about them? They are recorded in our Statute Book, like other matters of equal importance, and are the objects of ferious ftudy and contemplation; precedents that are regarded with reverence and with gratitude towards thofe who made them, but which we hope never to have occafion to follow. Thefe are the fentiments which are fuggefted by good sense on the view of thefe valuable memorials; and as they are never thought of without fome mixture of concern and pain, we are always glad to lay them afide, and we rarely wifh to recall them.

But what manner of men muft they be who make this a fubject for Tavern Meetings, for congratulation, and for frivolous feftivity! a fubject to declaim, to combine, to run ftark mad upon! However, they know their meaning, and there are very few of us who do not know their meaning alfo. All this wondrous paffion is excited by the *idea* of a Revolution; what they *idolize* is a *Revolution in the abftract*; and *thefe Revolution* principles are the only ideas they profefs of our Conftitution.

But.

BUT we muſt not expeſt men to be ſo void of caution as to avow ſuch a motive; *they* pretend nothing more than the ſame event which we all mean; and, upon ſuch a conſideration, *they* think themſelves juſtified ſufficiently in all they ſay and do. To repeat nothing here of the folly in ſuch effervefcence of zeal, I wonder, conſidering the rank and ſtation of ſome of theſe perſons, that a ſenſe of good-breeding and decorum has never ſuggeſted to them that ſo much commemoration of that Revolution, repeatedly urged out of all ſeaſon and meaſure, cannot ſound agreeably in the ears of the Sovereign. To him, ſuch commemoration muſt convey ſome inſinuation of reproach. I know, ſome who have had qualms of this ſort, have excuſed themſelves by alledging that *The Hanover Succeſſion* aroſe in conſequence of the *Revolution.*

BUT with the good leave of theſe Gentlemen, the way for *them* to manifeſt ſuch ſentiments would be expreſsly to commemorate *The Hanover Succeſſion;* for which I never heard that, in all their zeal, they had formed one Club, or made one dinner. And it does not look well, that when they are gratifying their own prejudices and pre-poſſeſſions in poſitive and plain terms, they ſhould compliment their Sovereign only by circumlocution, and leave him to make it out himſelf, as he can, by collection and inference.

G

SUPPOSE, for a moment, that fome Patriot fhould, among the eftates that he has not yet been obliged to fell, poffefs one that came to his anceftor from the favour of the Crown (which is no obftacle to the defcendants being Patriots), and that this eftate had come to the Crown, as perhaps it may again, by forfeiture for high treafon; if fome wag of a tenant fhould collect a noify meeting in the village to celebrate there the virtue of *forfeiture and confifcation for treafon*, and alledge a reafon like the above, I doubt whether the circumlocution would give much relifh to the joke in the mind of the faid Patriot. But it is not for men of a popular difpofition to do by others as they would be done by; they are men who do no right and take no wrong; men who reap where they fow not. Like the Patriots of former times, the godly *Puritans, they* have a privilege peculiar to themfelves, that difpenfes with the obligations which bind ordinary perfons, who are not *of the Brethren.*

BUT though the term *Revolution* throws confufion on the nature of the event it is meant to denote, it muft yet be confeffed, that it is not wholly without analogy to the circumftances attending it. As this term is of a comprehenfive and loofe import, and of a capacity for the worft

men

men to find their own meaning in it, fo that event, which was brought about by the energy, good fenfe, and firmnefs, of fome of the beft and greateft men in the Nation, was of a nature (unlike moft good things) to be helped on by the concurrence and approbation of fome of the worft men that could be found. But there was this difference between the two defcriptions of agents; what was merit in the one clafs of men was none in the other. Thofe who loved the antient Government, and knew the value of Monarchy, had great prepoffeffions to facrifice before they could take fuch a ftep, though for the prefervation of both, and though they knew that on the prefervation of both depended their Laws and Liberties. But the reft, who had no partiality for Monarchy, or who were ignorant or carelefs of its value; the *Republican*, the *Prefbyterian*, and the *Sectaries*, to whom may be added a long train of the abandoned and diffolute; nothing was more eafy to them than to join in any thing that looked like fuccefsful rebellion. Thofe who hated the very frame of the Government could not but be pleafed with the fhock it now received: fome hoped that the change might lead to other innovations; thofe who had been ufed to pull down and deftroy, gladly faw a profpect of reviving their old trade; perfons without a determinate

object

objeƈt were yet too much amûſed with novelty
not to be on the ſide of the authors of it.

WHATEVER were their motives for joining in
the new ſettlement, the *Republicans*, *Preſbyterians*, and *Sectaries*, did not fail ſoon afterwards
to urge their merit, and it muſt be confeſſed not
without ſome ſhow of reaſon. It was a fortunate
criſis to them; they now ſaw a Government which
they had a hand in rearing; they thought they
ſhould no longer be regarded with jealouſy and
ſuſpicion; and they hoped now to make themſelves a party *in* the State, inſtead of being conſidered as a party *againſt* it. Bending all their
endeavours to this point, the firſt thing to be done
was to get a good name. For this purpoſe, they
took their ſtand among *The Whigs* : under the
pretence of that way of thinking, they began to
vent their political opinions; which, however,
they now ſo tampered and turned as to adapt them
to the Government eſtabliſhed by Law. As they
ſacrificed the rigour of their own notions, they
did not fail to take a ſimilar liberty with the principles of the Government; and ſo they have gone
on, from thoſe times to our own, corrupting the
genuine principles of the Engliſh Laws and Government, in order to ſuit them to their own theories and ſyſtems, till they have filled the whole with
uncertainty ;

uncertainty; and *The Conſtitution*, of which they are ſo inceſſantly debating, is made one of the moſt doubtful and difficult things to comprehend.

To theſe men, and to this ſiniſter deſign, we are indebted for the jargon of which I have juſt complained. *They* invented the term *Revolution*, to blind and miſlead; and they have never ceaſed repeating it, that they may put the People in mind of making another. This myſtery they have couched under the ſtill more looſe metaphyſical idea of *Revolution principles*; and by the glorious ſpell of—*The Conſtitution*—they can conjure up any form, faſhion, modification, reform, change, or innovation in Government they pleaſe, and it ſhall ſtill be nothing more, as they pretend, than the genuine true Engliſh Conſtitution.

THE term *Conſtitution* has nothing in itſelf objectionable: a plain man might receive it without ſuſpicion of any miſchievous implication lurking under it. It might be underſtood as a ſhort way of ſpeaking for—*The Conſtitution of the Government*. But thoſe who introduced this mode of expreſſion were men famous for doing nothing without deſign. That deſign was noted very early by perſons whoſe ears had been habituated to the proper language of our Engliſh Government.

It

It appeared to them, according to the language of one of them, " that this new term Conſtitution " was commonly brought forward with a Repub- " lican face, as if it meant ſomewhat excluding " or oppoſite to the Monarchy, and carried an " inſinuation as of a co-ordination or coercion " of the Monarchy*."

THE tenor of almoſt every thing that has been written or ſaid by this claſs of men, from that time to the preſent, on the nature of this ſuppoſed *Conſtitution*, juſtifies the ſuſpicions then early en-tertained. We need only recur to a few particulars to eſtabliſh and illuſtrate this character of them.

IT is from perſons of this way of thinking that we have heard the following curious obſervation, that " ſo and ſo, it muſt be confeſſed, is not war- " ranted by Law, but it is certainly a part of the " Conſtitution." To what illuſions a man's mind muſt be a prey before he can be brought to ac_ quieſce in ſuch folly! and how loſt muſt he be before he can have the boldneſs to vent it! I always thought, that it was the diſpoſition of Engliſhmen to require plain and defined ſen-tences for the Charter of their Rights and Liber-ties; that they claimed to have known, written,

* ROGER NORTH on the Engliſh Conſtitution.

and

and exprefs Laws to govern them; and that they
regarded high pretenfions founded on vifionary
and refined theories, as the air in which they were
built: and I thought, that *the divine indefeafible
Right of Kings*, with other fancies of former times,
were exploded principally, becaufe they were
pofitions that had no warrant from the known
exprefs Laws of the Land, but refted on general
reafoning, from topics not known to the ufage and
laws of the country : and I always believed, that
the fet of men who moft clamoured againft thofe
pretenfions, upon the very grounds here alledged,
were thofe who afterwards fet up this new fyftem.

BUT it feems to me, that this new fyftem, giving
origin to pofitions like that above mentioned, and
fo carrying the mind beyond the bounds of law
equally with the other, is quite as abfurd as the
former, and differs from it only in being much
more mifchievous. For whereas the former at-
tempted to raife the imagination to fomething
above us, which might footh and elevate the
fenfes ; the latter opens to us no fpace wherein
the imagination can exercife itfelf, but the very
gulph of Democracy, there to toil and turmoil,
without hope of reft or confolation.

BUT as the Conftitution was alledged, upon
this fyftem, to be fomething that differed from
the

the Law and Government, it became neceſſary to have Profeſſors and Doctors to give reſponſes upon the nature of it, and direct our courſe in theſe untrodden paths. There accordingly ſtarted up a race of men called *Conſtitutional Lawyers.* I have heard it ſaid, that " ſuch a perſon is not " much verſed in the Law of Weſtminſter-Hall, " but he is nevertheleſs a very good Conſtitu- " tional Lawyer." As far as my obſervation goes, theſe Conſtitutional Lawyers ſeem to be divided into two claſſes. One of them conſiſts of Gentlemen who are bred indeed to the Law, but whoſe circumſtances are ſo competent that they are not obliged to make a livelihood of it; and as theſe Gentlemen need not torment their brains with the details neceſſary for the practice of Courts, they are at leiſure to extend the ſcope of their reading, and at liberty to take only the cream of their extended harveſt. As there is no compul- ſion, no preſſing ſtimulus to theſe purſuits, they are followed as it may happen ; and the principal objects propoſed to themſelves by ſuch ſtudents, are uſually matters relative to the King and Parliament. Such perſons often attain the cour- teſy of being called *Conſtitutional Lawyers ;* that is if they were ſentenced as ſeverely as I once heard *Gentlemanly Scholars,*—they are no Lawyers at all.

The

THE other clafs are of a very different·fort; they are really Lawyers; poffeffed of learning, experience, and parts, and, what is more, refolved to make the moft of them. Such perfons, having fecured their footing at the Bar, and being tolerably certain of preferving a lucrative practice, have nothing more to feek than preferment and rank. Thefe attach themfelves to fome Party in Parliament, ufually in Oppofition; they lend their name and credit to give ftability to the pretenfions of their Party; and they are too often ready to maintain, with colour of Law, every thing that needs fuch fupport;—*and verily thefe men* ufually *have their reward.*

BUT the *Revolution* politicians are much better able to explain their own doctrines than any of their Conftitutional Lawyers. A Gentleman of fingular wit and conviviality, who from accident and circumftances was, in fpite of his nature, made a Patriot, could not refrain from letting out the fecret. This Gentleman, I am fure, ought to be looked upon as an authority; for he enjoyed a longer career of popularity, of more violent heat and univerfality; and his name was more frequently joined with Liberty, (even to the becoming a by-word), than the beft of them, be his pretenfions what they may. This

H   Gentleman

Gentleman is said to have favoured us with a definition of that which had before puzzled so many; he gave a definition of the Constitution. He says—*The Constitution is every thing that is not Law.* And though he seems to have gone a little too far, in confessing for others, as well as for himself, he has also given us his idea of the class of Lawyers of which we have just been speaking: he frankly declared why he thought his learned friend and colleague, who was a great Constitutional Lawyer, so able and so valuable : " I think him," says he, " the best Lawyer in " Westminster-Hall; for he will make that to " be Law which I want to be so." And so much for *Constitutional Lawyers.*

But all who talk upon these subjects do not see so far, nor express their discoveries so clearly as this singular Gentleman has done. I verily believe, that among nine tenths of those who are so noisy for *The Revolution,* there are hardly two who agree upon the same conception of it. Most of them unite in repeating, " *The Constitution* " *as established at The Revolution.*" But whether by this they mean the precedent then established of removing one King and setting up another, which seems the most worthy cause for extravagant joy; or something about the dif-

penfing

penfing power, which however feems a little unim-
portant for fo famous a thing as a Revolution; or
fomething about Popery and Arbitrary Power,
which founds better, and is better for being general and indefinite ; or whether it is not fomething
divided into chapters and fections, detailing a
new fyftem of fuperfine texture, differing from.
that which prevailed in the popifh and arbitrary
reigns of Charles II. and James II.: whether
any thing like thefe, or what elfe has poffeffed the
brains of thefe men, when they declare themfelves
friends of " *The Revolution, and the Conftitution*
" *then eftablifhed*," it is not eafy to collect.

BUT they will be very much furprized when
they are informed, that the matter about which
they make fo much ado, is fomething very different from what they expected and believed ; and
further when they fee it, they will, I promife
myfelf, think as lightly of it, as men of more fenfe
than they have long thought. Be it known,
then, to all thofe who have taken their " Con-
" ftitutional information" from Pamphlets and
Political Societies, that they have not yet looked
into the right place for the hiftory, nature, defign, and principles of this fuppofed Revolution.
But if they will read over Statute the 1ft of
William and Mary, Seffion the fecond, Chapter

the

the fecond, which is fhorter than any of the papers publifhed by the Societies for making Revolutions, they will find the whole fecret explained to them; to which, if they wifh a little more light, they may add Statute the 1ft of William and Mary, Seffion the firft, Chapter the fixth, which is ftill fhorter than the other.

It appears from the former of thefe ftatutes, that the Parliament, having placed King William and Queen Mary upon the throne, which King James chofe to leave vacant by his abdication, ftipulated nothing for the people but upon thefe points where King James had broken the Law, or what was underftood by the generality of men to be the Law of the Land. Indeed the nature of the cafe demonftrates this; for, if what he did had not been againft Law, he would have broken no truft, and the Parliament would have had no ground of complaint. There is only one exception to this; and that is, James being a Papift: *That* certainly was not againft any Law; but it was againft the difpofition of the Nation; and it was now the pleafure of Parliament that the King on the throne fhould be a Proteftant; which was accordingly in this ftatute provided for in future.

The

THE other points, which were twelve in number, were, as I have said, known to be the Law of the Land before, and were now declared and secured by exprefs definition in Parliament, only that what had been recent caufe of alarm, what was fo deeply impreffed on the minds of all, and what might be thought, from late experience, to be of a nature that required it fhould be folemnly inculcated, might be held up for admonition to future ages.

WHAT difappointment and difcomfiture it muft be to thefe idolizers of the Conftitution fuppofed to be eftablifhed at *The Revolution*, to difcover at length that they have beftowed their applaufe and affection upon the fhreds and patches of old date; and that if they had lived in thofe wicked reigns of Charles II. and James II. they would have enjoyed in theory, though not in practice (and *theory*, of the two, is more confidered by modern Reformers), as good a Conftitution as they have had fince, with the fingle exception of a Proteftant King.

BUT thefe vifionary zealots were referved for a difgrace more mortifying than this, and from a quarter where it was, to fay the truth, not deferved, and not at all to be expected. We live
in

in an age of *Conſtitutions ;* all the world are writing and talking upon Conſtitutions, and unfortunately too many have had opportunities to ſet themſelves at work to carry their idle ſpeculations into practice. What ſhould have happened in the natural courſe of theſe new events, when other countries were becoming free like ourſelves, but that the Engliſh Conſtitution, which had been held out as the famous original, ſhould now be placed at the ſummit of its celebrity ; and that the ingenious artificers, who had been working upon it ſo long to bring it to perfect poliſh, and had ſo tortured their brain for topics to ſet off its excellence and beauty, ſhould be ranked among the benefactors of Mankind ? But behold the periſhable fame of political theories ! At this moment of culmination and triumph ; the Conſtitution-makers of France and America, having arrived at ſuch ſkill in this trade as to outdo their maſters, turn ſhort upon them, and tell them,—" The Engliſh have no Conſtitution " at all !" and they follow up this aſſault by attacking *The Revolution* itſelf; queſtioning and reviling it in ſuch terms as if they would inſinuate, that we had no more of a Revolution than of a Conſtitution.

THIS was a blow that ſhould only have been felt by thoſe who had fabricated theſe idols, and

dreſſed

dreffed them out for their own worfhipping; but it muft be confeffed that it ruffled many men of a different way of thinking, who have ufed, as we all have, the term *Conftitution* without annexing to it any of the fanatical notions of its firft inventors. It moved their fpleen to hear *that* traduced and reviled, which they had fo juftly efteemed as the model for others to imitate; and this by Americans and Frenchmen! the firft having formed Conftitutions that looked like the mangled and degenerate members of ours; the latter propofing nothing to themfelves but a wretched imitation of thofe mifhapen and degenerate productions.

A LITTLE reflection, however, prepares us to give an anfwer to thefe miferable but prefumptuous pretenders.

THE above writers on *this* fancied Conftitution had been employed to exalt its theoretical perfection, and had worked up certain general pofitions which they laid down as fundamental principles of the Conftitution. When many imaginations were engaged in the fame purfuit, a diverfity of fpeculations was to be expected: pofitions were oppofed to pofitions, and terrible was the conteft to fettle what were and what were

not

not the true Principles of the Englifh Conftitution. When the Americans came to the bufinefs
of erecting a fettled Government, it was natural
for them to call to mind this controverfy in England; and to take warning from this fuppofed
defect in our Eftablifhment. They refolved
therefore, above all things, to guard againft the
like uncertainty in their own. They accordingly
began the formation of their Governments by lay-
ing down certain fundamental principles, com-
prifing a Conftitution in the abftract, antecedently
to their commencing the building in fubftance
and detail. The French have taken the fame
courfe in the regeneration of their Government.
Thefe men, therefore, might very well, though
not very handfomely, tell their mafter-workmen
in this country that we had no Conftitution; that
is, that thofe fundamental principles, which had
been fo long vaunted, were only the theories of
private men; had no authority, no public fanc-
tion; and were all of them denied by one or other
amongft ourfelves; whereas, on the contrary,
they had a Conftitution which they could fhew,
drawn out into plain and clear pofitions, acknow-
ledged by every one, forming the bafis on which
the Government was erected, and furnifhing an
unvarying regulator, by which the Government
might

3

might be fet right as often as it fhould happen in practice to deviate from them.

But thofe amongft us who had never given their minds to fuch reveries might, without yielding any thing, have taken thefe Conftitution-makers at their word; and at once allowed that we had no Conftitution in the fenfe in which *they* underftand it. As many of them as were Englifh and Americans had been told this often before; they knew well and long ago that their conceits about Conftitutional knowledge were confidered either as illufion or impofture, contrived to ferve the temporary purpofes of a Party, and reprobated by moft men of fenfe in the Kingdom.

In fhort — The *Government* we know — and the *Laws* we know—but the *Conftitution* we know not.—It is an unknown region, that has never been vifited but by dreamers, and men who fee vifions; and the reports they make are fo contradictory, that no one relies upon them. Yet we can manage to fpell out of them, that there is refident there a great deal of faction and fedition; envy and ambition; and fomething that looks like eternal warfare of Party. But the Englifh Government is real and fubftantial; we fee and feel it; we can take its height and its depth;

I   and

and we know its movements, becaufe they are regulated by eftablifhed and known Laws. This is the only Conftitution ever fuppofed or named by men of fober minds and found underftanding; that is, *the Conftitution of our Government,* or *the Conftitution eftablifhed by Law.*

HAVING faid fo much upon this fuppofed Revolution, and the Conftitution faid to be formed upon it, I cannot pafs over a Party amongft us, which I have already named, and which had a confiderable hand in the tranfactions we have juft reviewed. Of the *Whig Party* in general, and of the whole of their conduct, I fhould feel much difficulty in giving an opinion. To fay the truth, they are believed by many to have done fo much fervice, and by many more to have done fo much mifchief, I know not how to appreciate them. But I have no other concern with their conduct than as they took a part in the defign which has been carrying on fo many years, for corrupting the minds of men on the fubject of our Government and Laws, and in fomenting the diforders that have been wrought by mifreprefenting what *they* call *The Revolution,* and the *Conftitution* fuppofed to have been *then eftablifhed.*

THIS,

THIS, like every other Party, may be viewed in two lights. In the firſt place, they were a ſet of men who agreed to make a common cauſe, and ſtand by one another in public affairs; and the ſingle object they propoſed to themſelves was, to force the preſent holders out of power, and to force themſelves in. But this would not go down with people of ſenſe who looked on; and as *they* had a great ſway, though not always ſeen, in balancing the weight of Parties, they muſt be won by ſome profeſſion of principles that ſounded well, and promiſed ſomething for the benefit of others than the profeſſors of them. Every ſet of public men muſt, therefore, in the next place, have a ſet of public principles. Upon theſe principles they very liberally and frankly declare, when out of office, they mean to act; and it is taken for granted they will adhere to them when poſſeſſed of power. A party thus furniſhed with principles, ſets out in its purſuit of power, and opens that ſcene which is daily rehearſing in this country, to the annoyance and miſery of all, both actors and ſpectators. I verily believe there is not a partizan, who in his cloſet can review the planning and plotting, the clamor and ſtruggles, the ſhifts and artifices, of the day, without compunction and ſhame. There is not a man of *Good Senſe* in the Kingdom but

I 2   has

has been so sickened with the disappointments from great undertakers in Party, as to be brought to regard the pretensions of public leaders little otherwise than as the strutting and fretting of so many Players upon the Stage. But this belongs to all of them, and is not peculiar to the *Whigs.*

WHEN the Government was settled on King William, the Whigs had very just title to consideration; for though they were not the principal persons who brought about that event, the scale being turned by another description of persons high in Church and State, yet they were the first who suggested the measure: they had begun it by the Exclusion-Bill in Charles the Second's time; they had never ceased driving on the same design till it was accomplished; and therefore, besides the merit of activity, they had that of foresight; having so long ago predicted that James would not be borne on the Throne, and that the only measure was to exclude him from it. The memory of what was past gave weight and importance to the Whig Party, and they immediately gained an ascendancy, which, by one means or another, was more or less maintained afterwards for many years.

ALL

ALL this was not compaſſed without the aid of certain public principles, which were made the creed and teſt of the Party. What ſo natural for Whigs as to conceive a ſet of principles ſuggeſted by the recent event in which they had ſuch a ſhare, and took ſo much pride; and what more likely to be well received, and become generally popular, than opinions that were to make the Nation ſatisfied with what had juſt been done, and ſhew that the Settlement then made, and the principles on which it proceeded, were founded in the cleareſt reaſon and wiſdom! Having ſo ſtrong an intereſt in keeping the eyes of the Nation fixed on that event, they went great lengths for the advancement of theſe opinions. Hurried on by the heat of party and of the argument from one topic to another, they at laſt entangled themſelves in theories and ſpeculations which did not properly belong to them, and which they could not view with ſatisfaction. They were, probably, precipitated into theſe difficulties by the dangerous politicians before deſcribed, who were received into the Party, and who, by theſe means, under the name of Whigs, were, in all their writings, promoting their darling object of a Republic.

THERE is too much facility in all Parties to admit among them any one who will join in the

cry,

cry, and contribute in any way to support the cause. Whether the Whig Party held themselves out more than any other for receiving partizans, or their principles were more congenial with those who were prone to hazardous experiments on the Government and Laws of this Country; perhaps both these might operate in producing the effect; but certain it is, that the Whig Party has contained in it some of the most dangerous men, and produced some of the most pestilent writings, that have appeared. No man, however averse to our Government, but has had the confidence to call himself a Whig; no writing so mischievous and seditious, but the Writer of it has justified it upon the principles of a *Whig*, and the principles of *The Revolution*.

But, notwithstanding the exceptionable parts of some of these Writings, it is certain that the constant hammering of the same matter had the effect of producing a great deal that passed current in the world. The principles of the Whig Party being very comprehensive and loose, some approaching to one extreme and some to the other, could not fail of gratifying a variety of palates, and by the force of one or the other, the Party made a number of friends, and grew to be very powerful in every respect.

THEY

THEY were aided, however, by fomething as powerful as opinions and political theories. The acceffion of the HANOVER FAMILY to the Throne firft gave this Party a decifive fuperiority over their rivals: and this is a circumftance in the hiftory of the Party that deferves to be remarked; for notwithftanding they met, upon the whole, with little countenance from their Hero King William, and indeed fuffered a rebuff, that, with their expectations, muft have been a great difcomfiture to them, and certainly funk deep into their minds; and although, during the reign of Queen Anne, they were never entertained by her but againft her will, fo that they never eftablifhed themfelves completely as a reigning Party till the time of George I. and after they had once got that footing, they were permitted to retain it for a great length of time: I fay, confidering all this, it is remarkable that, in their Commemorations, they fhould have nothing more to beftow on the Hanover Succeffion, than what I had occafion before to notice, and that they fhould keep all their demonftrations of regard for King William alone.

BUT if this conduct has not fhewn their gratitude, it has fhewn another thing, namely, that the profeffion of Party principles is thought by them a more firm dependence than the obligations of

per-

perfonal attachment; and that they have been men
fo wife in their generation, as to prefer what they
thought was moft to be relied on.

But during the reigns of George I. and
George II. the Whigs, for the moft part, had
an unbounded and uninterrupted fway; and
during all that time it was impoffible but thofe
termed Whig Principles fhould have the afcen-
dency. All other Parties were at that time under
fufpicions or out of credit; Loyalty and Whiggifm were like fynonimous terms; and who could
difpute the foundnefs of opinions that were
named from the men who were entrufted by their
Sovereign, and bore fway in all parts of the
Kingdom? Added to this, a certain conceit had
obtained, that Political and Civil Liberty depended upon the very principles profeffed by this Party; that they were neceffary conclufions from the
enlightened philofophy of the times; that they
were upheld and illuftrated by the writings of the
moft eminent among the fearchers after Truth;
and that they were likewife in unifon with all the
beft times of Roman and Grecian literature, whofe
remains were the ftudies of our youth, and the
ornament and delight of our riper years.

All thefe ftrong inducements, whether from
the power of the Party, or the dazzle of their
principles

principles united, concurred in giving great authority to any thing that bore the name. The
Whig Party was the receptacle for all thofe who
belonged to no other Party, or had not given
themfelves the trouble to prefer one fet of political opinions to another, and yet did not like
to belong to nobody: in the fame manner as
thofe who are of no fect, and have not bufied
themfelves about religious opinions, are fuppofed
to belong to the Church of England. Time was,
that a man of a quiet fpirit, who did not like to
expofe himfelf to cavil or queftion, would be
afraid not to profefs himfelf a Whig: it muft be
fomething wrong in the head or the heart that
could induce a man to think otherwife than as a
Whig!

But the empire of opinion, like others, will
have its end, and when things are come to the
extreme, a change muft be expected. Men
who were contented, as times went, to pafs for
good Whigs, did not like to be refponfible for
all the fophifticated opinions that were imputed
to the Party; and many caft about to find fome
decent way of alleviating the yoke they were
under, without flying out into open revolt againft
their old friends. Some of thefe difcovered the
diftinction of *Conftitutional Whigs*, by which they

K   did

did not mean the Conftitution in the fenfe of the
Whigs, which would have been to exprefs *idem
per idem*, and would have been a diftinction without a difference, but the Conftitution in the fenfe
in which all other men have ever underftood it;
and it was the fame as if they had faid—" We
" are Whigs, it is true; but we do not mean
" otherwife than well towards the antient Go-
" vernment and Laws of the Land."

THIS diftinction of *Conftitutional Whigs* made
an opening for a terrible fchifm in the
Party. It afforded an opportunity of feparat-
ing the good from the bad. But this could
not be expected to work exactly in fuch a manner. No man will write Rogue or Rebel upon
his forehead; and why fhould he pafs under
fufpicion, when it may be removed by a name
that nobody can prevent his affuming? Accordingly, as the Republicans before had no fcruple
to call themfelves Whigs, fo now not a Whig of
them but called himfelf a Conftitutional one;
and, confidering that *Conftitutional* had two fenfes, it fuited the latter as well as the former;
and, being of their own invention, it cannot be
denied, of the two, they had the beft title
to it.

4

BUT

BUT the principles of the Whigs were never so much put to the teft as when they came into the Adminiftration of the Government. It is a well-known complaint of them, that " the Whigs " in place always acted like Tories." This is certainly a juft remark, and in the nature of things it could not be otherwife; nothing can better fhew than this comparifon, how un-juftly the Party of Tories have been run down and exploded ; and, on the other hand, that the pretenfions of the Whigs are founded in no-thing but their own imaginations, and were totally incompatible with our Government and Laws.

FOR when the Whigs came into office, they found at Whitehall nothing of the *Conflitution*, and the *Revolution principles*, with which they had been ufed to amufe themfelves. They were to conduct a Government that had been formed long before their Party or notions were heard of; and they were to conduct it by the Laws of the Land, and the rules of office, that had long been the guides of practice, and could not fafely be changed or abandoned. For it is a fad truth to be told to thofe Gentlemen who are running the career of Oppofition with great eminence of talent and difplay of ability, that the object they

propofe

propofe to themfelves, as the reward of all their toil, is one of the dulleft affairs in the world. When they are in office they muft have done with mere words, and muft come to things; they muft fet down to work by line and rule; muft fearch Laws, hunt precedents, examine minutes of proceedings, confult and difcufs, and purfue a detail; often fubmitting themfelves to the advice of fubordinate perfons, who, though never heard of, do more perhaps to keep the machine a-going than their principals.

This is but an humble employment for a perfon who has been ufed to work wonders with a fpeech, or a pamphlet, grounded on the *principles of the Conftitution as eftablifhed at The Revolution.* But this, among other proofs, fhews the truth of what has been contended, namely, That the Government and Laws are different from the vifionary Conftitution of which we have heard; and further, that this Government is fo compacted in all its parts, that every conceit of politicians muft vanifh before it; and that their authors, in fpite of all their theories, muft conform to the Eftablifhment defcended from their anceftors.

Happily

HAPPILY for us it has been found that, generally fpeaking, all Parties act on the fame principle when in office: this is well known, and
the cant of the time has been, to impute it to
tergiverfation and corrupt impreffions. But the
current of experience has been too uniform not
to difcover the true caufe of this. The government and Laws are too ftrong for any Party, and
all Parties muft conform to the eftablifhed order
of things. In the adminiftration of Government,
Party-principles are nothing, but perfonal qualification is every thing.———Where there is more
underftanding, more attention to bufinefs, and
more honefty, there, and there only, will the
Adminiftration be diftinguifhed from others, and
the Country feel the difference.

THIS way of thinking has gained ground
much of late years; and there has grown more
coldnefs than there ufed to be towards men who
meant to recommend themfelves principally by
their Party connexions. This change in the
public fentiment has had a confiderable influence
on the fortunes of the Whigs. They have long
funk in confideration as a Party, and the principles going under their name have become lefs
in vogue. At this time I doubt whether it is

more

more reputable to be thought a Whig, than some years ago it was to be thought a Tory.

But the finishing blow to all Party distinctions, and to the credit of all political principles that had no reference but to Party distinctions, seems to me to have been struck in the latter end of the year 1792. At that time an alarm for the safety of the Constitution as established by Law, which seemed to be threatened by the Republican party from within, assisted by the French Republic from abroad, roused the Nation as one man. All Party considerations immediately vanished before that of the common interest of us all. From that time the attention of all sober men has been fixed on the preservation of the Government and Laws; all former distinctions of Party are thrown aside, and the illusion of their principles is forgotten. There are now no divisions in the Nation, but that of the Friends to the Constitution as established by Law, and that of the Republicans, who are lying by for an opportunity to level every thing to the Equality of a French Democracy; and there are no political opinions by which men are distinguished, but those that are in favour of the Constitution as established by Law, and those who are against it.

Thus

THUS have I brought to a concluſion this Hiſtory of the Attempts to corrupt the old Engliſh
Conſtitution of Laws and Government. They
began and ended by the introduction of *French*
principles. We have ſeen how the *Puritans,*
educated in the ſchool of *Calvin* and other
French Proteſtants ſettled in Geneva and the
Low Countries, ſet out by queſtioning the Supremacy of the Crown, and the Government by Biſhops ; and, contending for a Democratic Government in the Church, taught the like principles
for the Government of the State ; inculcat-
ing the Natural Equality of Man, the Origin of
all Power from the People, and the Right they
have to call their Governors to account. We
have ſeen how theſe *Puritans,* under other names
of *Patriots, Preſbyterians, Republicans,* and *Sectaries,* in the time of Charles the Firſt, overturned
the Government in Church and State. We have
ſeen how they preſerved their principles after
they had an opportunity to mingle with the
Whig party, and paſs under that denomination ;
and laſtly, we have ſeen how a new ſet of Republican notions have been lately poured in upon
us from *France,* whence have been kindled new
flames of Democracy, which it is now the employment of every ſenſible man to keep under
and extinguiſh.

BUT

But though Party is deftroyed, Faction will remain ; and Whiggifm is not of a nature to lie quietly in its grave; its ghoft ftill haunts us, hovering round the fcenes of its former exhibition, and attempting, as well as it can in its prefent unembodied ftate, to act over again thofe parts in which it fo much delighted when in life and vigour. The only vifible appearance of the Party is in the *Whig Club*, which is the mere RUMP and refufe of the original; and, fuitably with its prefent contracted and diminifhed ftate, it confines its operations principally to the keeping up of an Election-intereft in Weftminfter.

I know that moft of the individuals of it compofe another Club, which holds certain Commemorations exprefsly with that defign. In fuch employments have terminated all the former importance of the *Whig Party ;* and, to make their fall ftill more confpicuoufly difgraceful, they have now a tail tacked to them of followers from the rout and rabble of Democracy; men, who have rendered the beft things odious by *their* corrupt contact; who have made the friendly appellation of *Citizen* a badge of feparation and enmity; and the very name of *Liberty* fufpected to the ear of an Englifhman. Yet they have admitted thefe men to cover the empty benches

at

at their meetings, and to partake in that communion of friendſhip, their eating and drinking, which is the ſtrongeſt teſt of approbation that can be given. This mixture of *Whigs* and *Democrats* muſt exhibit a ſtriking picture of the combination of Parties; to ſee the pride of the Ariſtocrat and the pride of the Democrat brought into ſeeming union, yet each determined to deſtroy the other, if the criſis for it ſhould ever arrive; to ſee the equality that prevails among ſo many diſcordant and imperious ſpirits ; the apparent conſent and confederation of all in one common cauſe! and then, in the ſame room, to hear a ſpeech from a man, on whoſe lips the aſſembled wiſdom of the Nation has hung with delight for hours, and afterwards to hear another from a *Citizen*, who comes from the Meeting of Democrats in the open air in St. George's Fields, to teach theſe Stateſmen and Members of Parliament what true Liberty is ! *

THE deſigns of theſe Democrats have been fully expoſed to the public view, on the trials of ſome of them laſt year for High Treaſon ; they were then indeed acquitted by a Jury, but they have ſince been *found guilty by their Coun-*

* At the Shakeſpeare Tavern, Oct. 10, 1795.

L

try, on the evidence of the proceedings at the trial, which are in the hands of every-body.

THIS new fet of Reformers pretend to have no other object than Univerfal Suffrage and Annual Parliaments: and they have chofen this pretence, firft, becaufe they muft profefs fome principles, that do not quite fpeak rebellion; fecondly, becaufe this fpecific project has been vented by fome men, not of the loweft confideration in any thing but the article of Good Senfe; and by others, not of the higheft in any thing but in their wealth and *rank*; thirdly, becaufe they knew (and we know too) that fhould they fucceed in carrying this point, the deftruction of Monarchy muft inevitably follow; and a levelling Republic may then be fubftituted according to the imaginations and will of this rabble.

BUT who are the actors that are moft diftinguifhed and forward in carrying on this defign? In truth they are of a defcription, that in other times would render them too contemptible to be the objects of dread; but in thefe days, when every thing debafed is to be extolled, and every thing noble and excellent is to be vilified and contemned; and when this has been actually exemplified among our neighbours, who promife

3   aid

aid to propagate this fubverfion among us; under
fuch circumftances, the very meannefs of the
caufe conftitutes the magnitude of the apprehen-
fion. The confidence we fee in them, cannot be
without great confcioufnefs of ftrength; and,
when the progrefs is all under ground, we may
hear the explofion before we have any knowledge
of the miners. The attempts of thefe *Reformers*
are all among the claffes of fociety, with which
we have neceffarily too little intercourfe. Artificers and handicraftfmen, journeymen and
apprentices in great manufacturing towns, are
wrought upon by furmifes of grievances, and re-
prefentation of remedies, which fet them a mad-
ding after politics and public affairs : this, with
an idea of their own importance, infpired by the
doctrine of unalienable Rights and the natural
Equality of Man, makes them uneafy in their prefent circumftances, and ready and on fire for any
change. This fever is kept up by their Clubs
and Affiliated Societies, in the *Jacobin* fafhion;
and by inflammatory publications, that are given
away or fold at a trifle, and that are difperfed
with incredible affiduity and in great numbers.
One principal object with them has been to feduce
the foldiery from their duty, by painting to them
their peculiar fituation in every way that could

poffibly

possibly generate dissatisfaction and insubordination.

THESE are the lowest orders in this herd of politicians; and as they are the corrupted and misled, they call, perhaps, more for our pity than severe condemnation. But the corruptors, those who are the professors and missionaries of Sedition, are of a different class. These are men of a better station in life, but of a worse condition in mind; who, feeling nothing but discontent and turbulence in their own bosoms, would willingly light up a general confusion around them; men bankrupt in their purse or their character, who cannot be worse circumstanced than they are, and see no hope but in a Revolution; whose parts have been meliorated by education and sharpened by necessity; able to perform much, and ready to undertake any thing; knowing the world and the ways of it; with activity, and the gift of speech; agitators, always in action or preparing for it.

WHAT may not be accomplished by the mischievous industry of such instruments, employed upon such materials? The topics to which they resort for persuasion, might mislead and captivate
those

thofe who had better underftandings than *their* auditors; indeed thefe profeffors declaim till the very orator is deceived himfelf. To tell men, that they are by nature equal to their fuperiors, and that the prefent inequality between them is brought about by oppreffion and tyranny;—to lay down, that the people may make and unmake the Government, and to tell the populace that *they* are the People;—in the hearing of the poor and neceffitous, to cenfure and vilify the rich and opulent;—to difparage thofe put in authority in the prefence of the evil-doers, to whom they fhould be a terror;—to make fport of the perfon and office of the King himfelf; and train the minds of men to a contempt of his authority and the Government they live under;—thefe are topics that are too congenial with the felf-love, the malice, and lightnefs of fome minds, not to be heard with approbation and applaufe; and they cannot long and repeatedly be declaimed on, fometimes in Political Clubs, and fometimes in Public Lectures, to a numerous auditory, without warping the beft difpofed to an habitual diflike for the Government, and a difpofition to attempt, or concur in any change that fhall be propofed; more efpecially if the change is to place them, as they believe, in a fituation to become their own Legiflators and Governors.

Such

Such is the defcription of the new *Democrats* who at prefent infeft the Country; a fet, who in the meannefs of their perfonal character, in the danger of their principles, and in the open profeffion of them, exceed every thing we have yet had in the nature of Party; a fet, that are not a Party, but a Confpiracy ; a band of Catilinarians, that look only for plunder and bloodfhed, general confufion and anarchy.

And thefe are the men with whom the *Refufe* of the *Whig Club* have fraternized to make a common caufe! the dregs of the upper claffes of fociety mingled with the dregs of the lower! This union cannot be viewed but with difguft and deteftation. If one of the parties meant to acquire patrons of their caufe, they are not to be blamed; and the getting into fo much good company is certainly an ornament that they needed. As to the others, the beft motive that can be afcribed to them is, that they meant to make ufc of thefe as partizans for ftrengthening their oppofition to the Adminiftrators of the Government. But this is a traffic that muft lofe them in character what they will never, by thefe means, recover in numbers. Whatever political men may think of fuch condefcenfions, they may affure themfelves, that difhonefty and impofture will not procure con-

fidence

fidence to public men any more than to private; and that mean and unworthy connexions, formed upon no band of union but the bafe gains to be made by them, are equally difgraceful in public and in private life. And they fhould be told further, that fincerity and plain-dealing is ftill fo well liked, that I doubt whether, with all their mifchief, the political principles of one of thefe parties make them fo odious, as the moral principles of the other: men may hate the one, but the others they will defpife.

But I will not detain your attention any longer, at prefent. To exhibit the Conftitution of the Englifh Government in its true form; to feparate the corrupt gloffes and conftructions that have, from time to time, been impofed upon it; to expofe the pretexts of Parties; to take off the mafk from *Patriots* and *Reformers*; and to purfue the machinations of the *Jacobins*; thefe make an employment to which I fhall return in due time: and fuch *further Thoughts* I fhall addrefs to you. Thefe are matters, above all others, that call for the confideration of thofe amongft us, who are friends to order, love Quiet, and are poffeffed of the Good Sense by which Englifhmen are ufed to be guided.

AT

AT the prefent moment, YOUR attention will be fixed on an object of more immediate concern. The Parliament is now affembled. This is a feafon when your fuperintending influence is moft needed, and, we ufually fee, it is then moft happily predominant. But it is a feafon, when the fpirits of men, whether good or bad, are moft in motion; and all YOUR prudence is wanted to preferve us from folly and wickednefs.—You, therefore, YOU at leaft, WATCH.

October 29, 1795.

END OF THE FIRST LETTER.

www.ingramcontent.com/pod-product-compliance
Lightning Source LLC
Chambersburg PA
CBHW031453270326
41930CB00007B/979